THE
FIRST
CHRISTMAS EVE

ISBN 978-1-64468-407-8 (Paperback)
ISBN 978-1-64468-408-5 (Digital)

Covenant Books, Inc.
11661 Hwy 707
Murrells Inlet, SC 29576
www.covenantbooks.com

THE
FIRST
CHRISTMAS EVE

Kirk Jones

'T was the night before Christmas, and throughout Bethlehem,
Not a creature was stirring, not even a lamb.
Joseph and Mary, had traveled all day,
As night fell they looked, for a place they could stay.

In search of an inn, Joseph looked high and low,
But not one had a room, there was no place to go.
Now Mary with child, and feeling unable,
Would labor away, in a cold, lonely stable.

Alone and afraid, they soon filled with joy,
As Mary expecting, gave birth to a boy.
She looked to the sky, the stars shining bright,
Then gazed at sweet Jesus, and swaddled Him tight.

With the greatest of care, so as not to endanger,
She laid baby Jesus, down in a manger.
And the heavenly hosts, looked down where He lay,
As Jesus the Lord, fell asleep on the hay.

9

'Twas the night before Christmas, on the outskirts of town,
As the shepherds and sheep, were settling down.
Then an angel appeared, with a flash of great light,
Stunning the flocks, and causing great fright.

"Don't be afraid," said the angel above,
"For the news that I bring, is a message of love.
Glory to God, from the east to the west,
On Earth peace to those, on whom His favor rests."

'Twas the night before Christmas, in far eastern lands,
Began a journey of kings, across distant sands.
A sign in the stars, guided their trail,
Carrying gifts, from the lands that they hail.

Not even King Herod, could their journey deter,
To offer their gold, frankincense, and myrrh.
The praise that they carry, and the gifts that they bring,
Are a sign these wise men, know Jesus is king.

The night before Christmas, a story for all,
From shepherds to kings, God saw fit to call.

And He gave them His son, as a gift of salvation,
To every tongue, every tribe, every nation.

So when you think of Christmas, the greatest of gifts,
Is the blood that was shed, and the weight that it lifts.

God is the giver, He washes us white,
So Merry Christmas to all, and to all a good night.

ABOUT THE AUTHOR

Kirk Jones has written ten thousand different children's books in ten thousand different languages (five of those languages he invented himself). He always wakes up on the right side of the bed and has never skipped breakfast. He often kills two birds with one stone but is also known for killing two stones with one bird. Kirk has never cried during a Disney movie, not even *Bambi*, nor does he plan to cry during one in the future. He can sneeze with his eyes open and has successfully divided by zero on multiple occasions. Kirk takes the message of the Bible very seriously, but he clearly does not take himself too seriously.